Reviews

"A WONDERFUL BOOK… INSIGHTFUL… A book for all ages espousing the virtues and fun of the time honored family reunion."
—Ken Burkeen,
BLACKVOICES.COM

"An entertaining way of teaching children to value family."
—F.M. Avey, author of *The Harlequin Nutcracker, Girl Gifts*

"In just a few short pages, *The Family Reunion Is Not a Real Vacation* took me down memory lane to my own family reunion as a child and as an adult. Valerie Rose connected the dots in showing children how family reunions truly can be a real vacation."
—Sandra King Freeman
Soulful Crosswords

Dedication

Dedicated to my Mom and Dad, Daisy and Elzie and to my darling daughters, Samantha and Taylour. But especially to Samantha whose inquisitive nature lead her to ask the question, "Mommy, when are we going to go on our *real* vacation?" Which ultimately inspired a significant portion of this book.

In memory of Renee J. McCall.

Triangleheads

The Family Reunion Is Not A *Real* Vacation

Written by Valerie Rose

Illustrated By Samuel J. Simmons

This material is protected by US copyright laws.
Copyright © 2001 Valerie Rose
Graphical Concept Copyright © 2000 Valerie Rose
Post-Illustration Copyright © 2000 Valerie Rose
Post-Illustration by Samuel J. Simmons

All rights reserved. No part of this book may be reproduced or transmitteed in any form or by any means, electronic or mechanical, including photocopying, recording or by any information storage and retrieval system, without the written permission of the author, except by a reviewer who may quote brief passages in a complimentary review.
For information on permissions contact Roses Are READ Productions.

Summary: Unusual twins Sam and Tay, inform their parents that they do not want to go to the family reunion because they instead want to go on a *real* vacation. The two learn that the family reunion is not only a *real* vacation, but also much more.

ISBN: 1-931646-00-7

Library of Congress Catalog Card Number: 2001090185

Printed in the United States.

Beaver's Pond Press, Inc.
5125 Danen's Drive
Edina, Minnesota 55439-1465
Phone: 952-829-8818
Fax: 952-944-4065
E-mail: info@beaverspondpress.com
Website: www.beaverspondpress.com

in association with

Roses are READ Productions
P.O. Box 7844
St. Paul, MN 55107
E-mail: valerie.rose@gte.net
Website: www.valerierose.com

Acknowledgements

I would like to thank the Creator.

I would like to thank my parents, Elzie and Daisy. Especially to my mother, who always stressed the importance of our family reunion.

I would like to thank all of my family and friends for their love and support.

I would like to thank Samuel J. Simmons, who took my simple graphical concept and exploded the Triangleheads, the Ovalheads and the Diamondheads into life via his beautiful illustrations.

I would like to thank Portland Jones who designed this book. Portland, I don't know what I would have done without you.

I would like to thank Milt Adams and Jack Caravela for their direction and expertise.

I would like to thank Adrian Crawford, who designed the Roses Are READ logo.

I would also like to thank André Thomas Consulting for providing a home for my website.

I would like to thank Mary Howard Buchanan of Buchanan Enterprises for her support and expert guidance, but mostly just for being a wonderful human being.

I would also like to thank all of my neighbors, who so many times cleared my snowy driveway. Special thanks to Mark Z., Lynn, Mark P., Liz, Bill and Gretchen.

I would also like to thank my fourth grade teacher, Ms. Jacquelin Patterson, and one of my fifth grade teachers, Mr. Ed Thekan, both of whom cared enough to take the time.

Hi! My name is Sam and my name is Tay.

And this is Zak and Mac.

We live in the Twin Cities.

That's in Minnesota, in case you were wondering. Minneapolis and St. Paul are two cities that are very close together. That's why they call them the Twin Cities.

They are alike in many ways, but at the same time they are very different. Just like us!

Welcome to the Triangleheads Family Reunion

Every year we travel to a different city to go to the family reunion.

A family reunion is when people who are in the same family come together in one place to see each other, hug each other and be happy.

We love to see our family, but this year, the family reunion is in Gulfport, Mississippi.

Gulfport, Mississippi is really far away from our house.

So Dad told us that this year, we are only going to go on one vacation.

This year, we are only going to go to the family reunion.

But we want to go on a *real* vacation.

When we were little babies, our Mom and Dad told us that we could talk to them about anything.

When we have a problem, we talk to them because sometimes they can fix the problem.
So we are going to talk to them about this.

Do you want to see how you can fix a problem by talking to your Mom and Dad?

Good!

Come with us.

"Mom, Dad, we want to know when we are going to go on our real vacation."

Mom and Dad looked at each other curiously. "What do you mean, real vacation?"

"Well, Cheryl and Daryl Ovalhead are going to Jamaica in June," said Sam.

"And the Diamondheads are going to Hawaii next month," added Tay.

"Yes, and we are going to Gulfport for the family reunion," Mom said.

"Yeah, but we want to go on a *real* vacation," the twins chimed together.

"The Family Reunion is a *real* vacation," Mom and Dad said together.

"Uh-Uh," Sam and Tay protested.

Hawaii

"Aloha!"

Dad gave Mom a secret wink. "Okay, why don't you tell us what a *real* vacation is," Dad said. "Then you can tell us what a family reunion is and we can compare the two. Okay?"

"Okay, Dad."

"Well," Sam said, "on a real vacation, we go to a nice hotel, we eat out everyday, people are nice to us, we play with other kids, we float in the swimming pool, and we can relax in the whirlpool."

"Yeah, and a *real* vacation has vacation trees!" Tay added.

"Yeah," Sam said, "and a *real* vacation has a beach and we can play in the sand, and we can swim in the ocean."

"You girls were pretty young the last time we went to Gulfport," Dad said, handing them a set of pictures. "But you see, Gulfport has a beach and sand." Sam and Tay looked at the vacation pictures and then at each other.

"What else do you do on a *real* vacation?" Mom asked.

"We fly on the airplane!" Tay said.

"And we go to museums, shows and to the zoo!" Sam said.

"And we can go on a boatride!" Tay yelped.

"Yeah...a real vacation has everything!" They chimed together.

"Anything else?" Mom asked.

"Well, no. Guess not."

Dad gave Mom a secret wink. "Oh, I see the problem. When you go to the family reunion you don't get to ride on the airplane."

"Well, no. I mean yes," Sam said, "I mean Gulfport is too far away from our house, Dad. We have to ride the plane to get there."

"Oh, I know," Mom joined in, "when you go to the family reunion you don't get to stay at a nice hotel."

"Well, no. I mean yes, but—" Tay said, slowly, hesitating.

"Okay, girls, why don't you tell us what you do at the family reunion. Maybe that will make it easier for you to talk about, okay?"

DAD and MOM

SAM and TAY

"Okay Dad," they said together.

"Well, on Friday we see Mama Daisy and Granddaddy."

"And Jecora and Janel and Shay and Jazmine and Austin and NiNi and all of our relatives that we haven't seen in a long time," Sam said.

"And we give them a big hug," Tay added.

"On Friday night we swim in the hotel swimming pool."

"Yeah, we dive to the bottom and float on our backs," said Tay. "That's our favorite." The girls let out a silly giggle.

"On Saturday, we visit the mall or go to the zoo," Sam said.

"We laugh, play, dance and smile," said Tay.

"On Saturday night we eat snacks and cake and dance at the family party. Sometimes we have African dancers and drummers."

"On Sunday, we eat. Then we have church. We give praise and thanks," Sam said.

"We see pictures and listen to stories about Great, Great Grandma Martha, Great Grandfather Clarence and Great Grandmother Rosalee."

"After we have church, we give gifts to the youngest and oldest Trianglehead at the reunion."

"We laugh, play, dance and smile," Tay added.

"And on Monday we have a picnic at the park!"

"Hmmm..." Mom and Dad said together.

"Oh, I see the problem," said Dad. "On a real vacation you have lots and lots and lots of fun. And you can't have lots and lots and lots of fun at the family reunion because you have to learn about your family history and you are always with people in your family who you love and who love you right back."

DAD and MOM

Sam and Tay turned to each other and began to think. While they were thinking, Dad gave Mom a secret wink.

The two girls turned back to their parents.

"Mom, Dad," they chimed together, "I guess they are the same. A family reunion is a *real* vacation after all! They are alike in many ways, but at the same time they are different, just like us!"

DAD and MOM

SAM and TAY

"That's right girls," Mom said. "That's exactly right."

About the Author

Valerie Rose is the owner of Roses Are READ Productions and the author of several books. She lives in Minneapolis, Minnesota with her two children.

❏   Yes! I want to order more copies of *The Triangleheads and The Family Reunion is Not a Real Vacation*

Print price: $12.95 US / $14.95 Canada
Shipping: $2.95 per book (US)

Mail your check or money order with this completed order form to:

Roses Are READ Productions
Attn: Valerie Rose
P.O. Box 7844
St. Paul, MN 55107
e-mail: valerie.rose.@gte.net
websites: www.valerierose.com or www.thetriangleheads.com

    Quantity: _____

    Price: _____

    Tax (MN residents
    only, 6.5%): _____

    Shipping: _____

    Total: _____

Name: _____

Address: _____

_____

Phone: _____   E-mail: _____

Published by Beaver's Pond Press and Roses are READ Productions of St. Paul, Minnesota. Little Petals is the childrens division of Roses Are READ, an organization which produces and publishes books in all genres.